# THE AWESOME PHYSICS
## IN YOUR HOME

Written by **THE AMAZING THEATRE OF PHYSICS**
Illustrated by **TOMÁŠ KOPECKÝ**

Albatros

# DISCOVER PHYSICS...

FORCES

You know your own bedroom better than anyone else. You know where each toy goes, you know that you broke the chair, and you also remember how much it hurt when you fell out of bed. But do you know how the toys and the things in your bedroom work?

*I took it a bit too far – my heart nearly stopped.*

*Don't fall... Don't fall...*

## Center of gravity

Everything around us has one point that we call the center of gravity. When we know where it is, it's easy to know when a thing will fall and when it'll stay put. Try it with this book. As long as the center of gravity is above the table, it won't fall. As soon as you slide the book towards the edge of the table, though, shifting its center of gravity into the air, the book will fall to the floor.

the center of gravity of a book

the center of gravity while doing a bridge

the center of gravity of a ring with a stone

## When will it fall?

Regularly shaped things like a sheet of paper or a book have their center of gravity in the middle. A ring also has its center of gravity in the middle, even though nothing is actually there. And we humans have our center of gravity somewhere near our belly button.

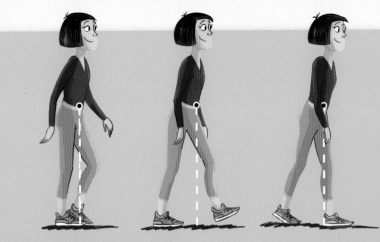

## Rocking on a chair

Do you like rocking on your chair? Just be careful you don't fall backwards. You always have to rock so that your center of gravity doesn't shift beyond the back legs of the chair. Our center of gravity always has to be above the point of contact with the ground – otherwise we will fall.

## Balance in every step

It's the same with walking. When you are standing, your center of gravity is above your feet. When you are walking, you tilt your center of gravity away from your foot and you are falling until you get back over the other foot. Walking is really just a series of controlled falls. Cool, right?

## A flywheel toy car

And then there are flywheel cars. With these you have to first rotate the wheels in the direction you want the car to go. Then, with the help of some cogs, these rotating wheels turn a heavy wheel called the flywheel. The flywheel then keeps turning for a long time and helps to keep the car moving for a fair distance, even across the whole of your bedroom. You've probably heard of a flywheel before – they are used in lots of other devices. Satellites even take them into space to help them steer.

Mine winds up in reverse.

## A spring-loaded toy car

Some toy cars move by themselves even though they don't have batteries. How do they do this? There are two possible ways. The simpler one is a spring-loaded toy car – that's the kind you have to pull backwards. The spring inside is wound up, transferring energy to some cogs that spin the car's wheels quickly forwards. The further you pull the car backwards the faster it'll go forwards.

We load a spring like this...          ...and a flywheel like this.

## How are colors made?

The world is colorful, and that makes it cheerful and beautiful. Right now you are looking at the page of a book, where light you see is all reflected, but whenever you look at a screen, it shines by itself. Is there a difference here?

Yellow is the base color.

### How to mix the right color

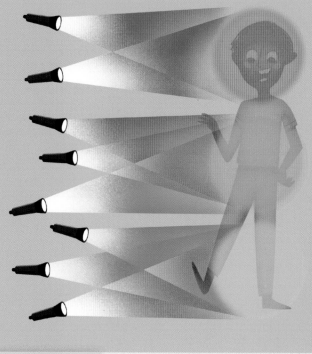

## A color experiment

On a piece of tissue paper, draw a series of colored dots in a row using dark water-based markers. Then dip the bottom of the tissue into water. The water will start to climb up the tissue and the colors will run. You will see that some of these lines will run into different colors. Black, brown, and even purple should come out nicely.

LIGHT

## Let's paint

When you paint with tempera paint (a kind of fast-drying, colorful paint) or watercolors, the more paint you add, the darker the color you get. That's why the most common color used by painters is white. They mix it with other colors to get different shades.

Painters like to have as many shades as possible, but they could actually make do with just blue, red, and yellow. These are the primary colors, which they then combine with each other and with black and white. In fact, house painters do something very similar when they add a small amount of paint to white to get the shade they want.

So many new shades!

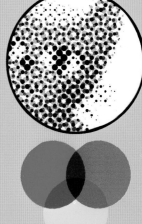

## Printing colors

A printer's palette of colors is different from a painter's. This palette is not even the same as the one you see on a computer screen. If you open up a printer and look inside, you'll find yellow, magenta, cyan, and also black. A printer doesn't need white because it prints onto white paper. Under a microscope, a printed sheet looks like a mass of colored dots.

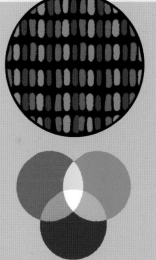

## Colors on a screen

Have you ever looked at a screen through a magnifying glass? Try it out with a computer, a TV, or even a cell phone. If you don't have a magnifying glass, place a tiny drop of water on the screen. You'll see small dots that we call pixels. If we were to magnify them under a microscope, they'd look something like this. The shape of the pixels is different on different screens, but you will always find three colors there: red, green, and blue. But why these three?

When we mix the red, green, and blue colors of light on a screen, they make a brighter color together. This happens because computer screens find it hard to show dark colors, so when we mix these colors, they create a brighter result than the colors we started with.

## Let's mix lights!

The concept of primary colors is different when dealing with paints and pigments compared to when dealing with light. If we shine red light and blue light together, we get magenta. Red light and green light make yellow, and blue light and green light make cyan. And what about orange? We still just need our three primary colors, but we have to combine different strengths of light. To get orange you have to use less green but more red. And if you'd like lime green, then you'd need to use less red and more green light.

When everything is covered in snow, people usually fall into two groups. The first type rush excitedly outside and stay outside until they look like snowmen, while the second type prefer to watch the dancing snowflakes through a window. In either case, there is a lot to explore!

CHANGES OF STATE

## Magical icicles

Who would have thought that icicles needed heat? How are they actually formed? The warm house heats up the snow that has fallen on the roof, and it begins to slowly melt and drip down as if it's on a slide. It stops right at the edge of the roof, where it eventually freezes again.

STRUCTURE

## Unique snowflakes

No two snowflakes are alike. But they do have something in common. They all radiate out from the center in six directions. This is because they are formed from tiny crystals with six sides. Each one then falls to the ground by a different route, growing as it does so. Its final shape depends on how damp and cold the air it passes through is. So if you look at a snowflake through a magnifying glass, you can discover its whole life story!

Each snowflake is an original!

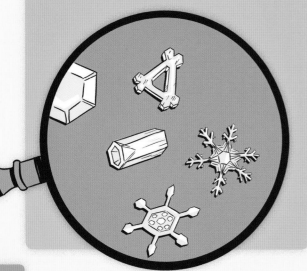

FORCES

## Inspiration from penguins

Uh-oh, a glacier... How do you cross its frozen surface without getting hurt? Try following in the footsteps of penguins, who have a lot of experience walking across ice. They take small steps and always tread carefully, putting their whole weight onto each foot. Your walk will have a funny wobble to it, but at least you'll be safe! Normally we take longer steps, which makes it easier for us to lose our footing.

## Does laundry dry in wintertime?

In summertime, all of our clothes dry perfectly, which is no big surprise. They are warmed by the sun's rays, which gradually makes the water evaporate. But what about in wintertime? Surely laundry will freeze in winter! But that doesn't matter. Ice can evaporate as well, and it doesn't even need to melt to do so, particularly on a dry, frosty day or if it's windy.

## How to make a cloud

Brr, it's cold! So cold you can see your breath. Has it ever occurred to you that you are actually creating your own small cloud just by breathing? Along with lots of different gases, you always breathe out a small amount of invisible water vapor as well. When you breathe out into the cold, the vapor transforms into water droplets, which we then see as a cloud. Clouds in the sky are formed in a similar way.

**HEATING**

## Is it cold there or not?

Dressing to go outside in winter can be quite tricky, and at times even a thermometer is of no help. Sometimes our teeth chatter when the temperature is freezing, while at other times it can be really freezing and yet we feel OK. How is this possible? The wind is to blame! When it begins to pick up, we immediately think it has gotten colder. This is because the wind blows away the layer of air that our bodies have heated up around us. And because our bodies then have to work hard to reheat themselves, we feel cold right then.

I want my layer of air back!!

# Look out for ice!

Snow, ice, and frost can cause many problems, especially in town, from minor inconveniences to major calamities. On the other hand, the frozen crystals are very beautiful. Quick, take a look before they melt...

winter tire

bike tire with spikes

tractor soles

Look out!

## Accident-free

We're not the only ones who slip and slide in wintertime – it happens to cars, buses, trains, and bikes... Whether it's snow or just a light frost on the ground, there's immediately a bigger risk of a bike skidding or two cars colliding. So how can we travel accident-free?

We put on winter boots, and we have winter tires for our cars. If you are one of those passionate cyclists who doesn't stow their bike in the garage in wintertime and rides to school or work, come rain or shine – or snow! – then you should try using tires with spikes. Don't worry, these spikes won't burst the tire – they point outward and dig into the ice, so the bike will skid less on the road. Mountaineers use the same principle when they attach crampons to their boots to scale steep glaciers.

## Ice cream experiment

What's that? Ice cream with salt? Yes! Don't worry, though. You can make ice cream from scratch using salt – but it won't taste salty. So let's get to it. Put some crushed ice into a large bowl and add salt. Then nestle a smaller bowl into the ice, pour in some cream, and sprinkle in a little sugar. Add whatever flavorings you want – cocoa or vanilla are always a safe bet. Mix it all together patiently and you'll soon see the results...

Salt the ice...

Cool the cream and sugar...

Safely to school.

## Clear your path

**WITH GRIT...**
We can make roads easier to drive on by adding grit. Even if there's only a small amount of grit, it helps create a slightly rough surface that makes driving smoother.

**WITH SALT...**
Why do they put salt on the roads? The kind of salt they use helps the snow to melt. Everything in the world has its own temperature at which it melts. Chocolate only needs a short time in the sun, while iron needs a blazing furnace. Snow only needs temperatures above freezing (32 degrees Fahrenheit) to thaw. Salted ice melts even in icy conditions – down to 5 degrees Fahrenheit.

**IS SALT REALLY MORE PRECIOUS THAN GOLD?**
Once it has served its purpose on the road, all of the salt flows into the town sewage system, along with the melted snow, but it also makes its way into rivers and streams and the surrounding meadows and forests. This is very bad for the environment, which is why we try to use salt on the road as little as possible.

## The secret of the winter flowers

How on earth does frost get on windows? Well, it cools the windowpane, which then cools the surrounding air. If the air in the room is damp, the water vapor can turn into droplets, which freeze on the cold glass. Instead of becoming snowflakes, they form gorgeous patterns.

**WHERE DO WE FIND THEM?**
These days, frost patterns can be seen mainly on the car windshields or old house windows. Most new windows are made from several panes of glass, so they no longer let in as much cold air. So these days, we don't see frost patterns at home as much . . . but we're a lot warmer!

**THE PRICE TO PAY FOR WARMTH**
Thanks to double- or triple-glazed windows, water droplets can drip onto the windowsill or the wall, sometimes causing mold. You can help prevent this, though, by cleaning and inspecting the windowsills and walls.

**A FINAL WORD OF ADVICE**
We have no choice but to open the windows frequently. Particularly in the kitchen after cooking, but also in the bathroom after showering.

Mix well...

Voilà! Homemade ice cream!

It might seem as if there is only empty air all around us, but the opposite is actually true. If we could see things that are invisible, we would be amazed at what this empty space is full of. It is filled with warmth, smells, and different sounds. For example, when someone says hello to you, they send soundwaves into the air, which make all of the surrounding air vibrate. There is also more light than we can see shining on us from the TV and from light bulbs, and the air is full of invisible Wi-Fi signals.

a selfie on Instagram...

storage for selfies and other data

Like!

Internet signal booster

Wow, she's looking good.

## Computer network

The internet is like a giant web made up of many smaller webs called networks. In the past, computers were only connected within one building or company. Later, they began to be connected across cities, countries, and even continents... and so the internet was born – a great computer network that connects the whole world. When you are browsing the internet, your computer sends a signal to other computers with different tasks. Some of them store data, others amplify this signal and process information. So, whenever you surf the web, you are connected to all other computers that are also "online".

And no more cold feet.

RADIATION

## A hidden source of heat

The heating in this room is hidden in the floor, which is why you won't get cold feet in here! The heat rises from the floor to the ceiling. Radiators, on the other hand, send warm air up to the ceiling, where it gathers. More and more molecules of warm air then arrive and push the slighter cooler ones downwards.

underfloor heating

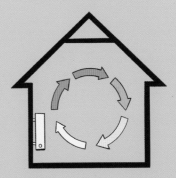

heating with a radiator

## The remote control

Changing the channel on the TV or adjusting the volume by pressing a button on the remote control is a piece of cake, right? But how does a remote control actually work? How does the television know exactly what we want it to do? It was easier for the earliest remote controls because they were attached to the TV by a cable. Today, though, the signal from the remote is transferred only by light. By pressing a button, you send a signal that makes a small flash of light. You can't see it, but the sensor on the TV recognizes the correct flash and changes the channel.

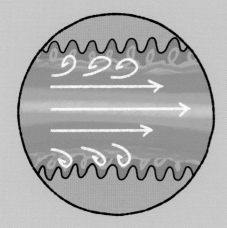

## The noisy vacuum cleaner

A vacuum cleaner blows a stream of air through itself, picking up dirt along the way. It sucks in air at one end and blows it out from the other end. This process is controlled, so you don't have to worry about sucking all the air out of a room! Vacuum cleaners are often annoyingly noisy. Most of the noise comes from the motor and the hose. Have you ever noticed that the hose of a vacuum cleaner always has grooves in it? Why is that? Well, when the air flows through the hose, small swirls form inside the ridges. These make the air in the hose vibrate and you hear a loud humming noise. If the hose was completely smooth, it would be lovely and quiet, but it could easily snap.

## Where does electricity come from?

No doubt you can name many things that use electricity. But try thinking about which devices are plugged in and which ones use batteries. Both ways of getting power are good and bad in different ways. Can you guess what they are?

Luigi Galvani

## Battery-powered

### THE FIDGETY FROG'S LEGS

It was a very interesting journey that led to electricity being stored in a battery, and it all began with some frog's legs. Yes, you read that right! One fine day, an Italian doctor and physicist named Luigi Galvani touched a frog's leg on a metal tray with his table knife and it twitched. After many experiments with frogs' legs, Galvani realized that electricity must be hidden within animals. And this twitch kick-started the development of a famous invention: the battery.

### AND WATCH IT FLOW!

Not long afterwards, another scientist, Alessandro Volta, discovered that animals were not actually needed to make electricity. We can create electricity when two specific metals touch each other. This was how Volta made the first battery – with discs made of materials called copper and zinc. Instead of frogs' legs, he placed flannel soaked in water between the cloth strips. Then all that was needed was to attach a lightbulb to the top and bottom of the column with wire and then electricity started flowing. Since then, the energy in electricity, which we call "voltage," has been measured in Volts in honor of Volta.

Ah-ha, electricity is concealed within animals!

Great Scott! Electricity is hidden in metals.

## Experiment with a remote control

At the front of a remote control, there's a mysterious flashing light that is invisible to the naked eye. We humans can't see it, but cameras can. That's because this light belongs to the infrared part of the light spectrum. Take a cell phone with a camera, or an actual camera, and flash the remote at the screen. If you're lucky, you'll see a red dot on it!

Alessandro Volta

# Plug-in

### ELECTRICITY FOR EVERY HOME

The invention of the battery allowed scientists to study electrical currents. They also discovered that it was possible to produce electricity in another way – with magnets. After nearly 100 years of in-depth research, scientists had a good understanding of electricity, but it was still a mystery to everyone else. Then a man named Thomas Edison invented the lightbulb. In order to get it into homes, he had to create all the other things a lightbulb requires. He built the first power station and power lines, invented switches, fuses, and a lot more. Quite the clever dude, right?

### THE FIRST SOCKETS

People got used to electricity very quickly. They even dreamed up tons of handy gadgets for the home. However, they didn't have any sockets to plug them into yet, because up until then, sockets simply hadn't been needed. Soon, though, the first electrical sockets began to appear across the world.

### SOCKET WARS

The very first electrical sockets were screwed into light fixtures. After that, anything could be plugged into them. However, each electricity company had a different shape for their electrical socket, and all of them were different. One socket in America was more popular than the rest. The people who made it tried to stop the other inventors from making it too. But in the end, they all decided to make this socket the one and only socket. And that socket is stillwhat we use today.

### SOCKETS FROM AROUND THE WORLD

Remember, only electrical appliances should be plugged into electrical sockets – it can be very dangerous to put anything else in them, so make sure to never do so!

### THREE COLORS OF WIRE

When you need to charge your cell phone, finding a plug is really important. A plug is like a special doorway for electricity to enter and leave your device. Imagine a magical bridge for electricity! Inside electrical cables there are three wires, each of which connects to one of the three holes you see in electrical sockets.

STRUCTURE

## Keeping dry

An umbrella, a raincoat, various waterproof things – all of these protect you from water, thanks to how tightly woven the material is. The smaller the holes in the fabric between the individual threads, the less chance water droplets have of getting inside. For a droplet to get through the small opening, it would have to divide into smaller droplets, which is very hard for it to do.

Waterproof materials don't let a drop of water through.

clothing that isn't waterproof

You might think that all of the things in the closet are supposed to keep us warm. But if you take a good look around, you'll find a lot of clothes that we wear for completely different reasons. Some of them protect us from the rain, others from the sun. Sometimes they are just fads, while other items make our lives easier.

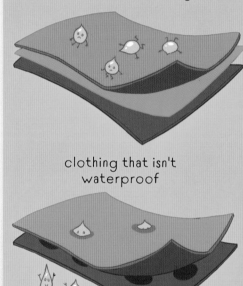

Great. It's warm and it looks good.

HEAT CONDUCTION

## Keeping warm

You often hear people say that a sweater "warms you up". And if we have cold feet, we put on "warm" socks. These phrases are slightly confusing. But why? Because it's actually you who is generating the heat! Clothes only keep your warmth next to you to stop it from escaping. This is called insulation. If you were to wrap an ice cube in a sweater, it wouldn't melt faster – in fact, the opposite would happen. It would stay cold because the sweater would insulate it from the warmth outside.

Still not melting, still not melting!

## Being seen

At night, many of us wear reflective strips so that cars can see us in the dark. They come in different shapes and sizes, and you can find them on lots of things. For example, take a look at your school bag – you might find some reflective strips there. When a car shines its lights on you, the reflective strip sends the light back towards them, as though you were shining a light at the car. The car can then easily see you. The next time you go out, don't forget to take something with a reflective strip on it. You'll be much safer because you'll be helping drivers to see you.

## Whiter than white

Have you ever noticed how white clothes can sometimes be dazzling? And every good physicist knows that they really are. This is because substances are added to white laundry that highlight the white color. They take some of the sunlight that is invisible to the eye and transform it into blue light, which you can see. This is why white pieces of clothing seem much brighter than they really are.

Aren't you roasting in that black t-shirt?

Yeah, but it's worth suffering for heavy metal!

glass

layer of metal

## A mirror

Have you ever noticed how strange the image in a mirror is? If you raise your right hand, it's your left hand that waves in the mirror. However, we've gotten so used to it that when we take a selfie on our cell phones the camera deliberately flips the image around like a mirror so as not to confuse us. In reality, mysterious mirrors – the ones here in the world, not on our phones – are just a highly polished piece of metal covered in glass.

## White or black

There is something unique about every color. You can see every smudge on a white T-shirt, while a black one makes you look slimmer. However, the two T-shirts are different in an even more important way. While the color white is good at reflecting light and heat, black absorbs a lot of it. So if you go for a walk in the heat of summer wearing a black T-shirt, you'll probably end up pretty sweaty. So think carefully about which color you pick.

## Do the clothes make the person?

They certainly do, and it's not just about fashion trends. Some clothes make it instantly obvious who is wearing them. You're bound to recognize the firefighter and the diver, but also the clothes worn by people who live in the desert. All of them wear the kinds of clothes that will help them as much as possible in the conditions they live or work in. And even if all of these clothes look very different, they all have one thing in common. They protect people from the heat or the cold, and they do this using air.

> Wow, so ice can also protect you against the cold?

### Air for staying warm

Air is really good at keeping things warm. It doesn't let heat pass through easily. To make the air hot, we have to use a lot of energy. So if we want to keep something warm on one side and something cold on the other side, we just need to put a layer of air in between. This is how windows with two or three layers of glass work, and it's also why our clothes help us stay warm.

### Inuits

People from the Inuit tribes (such as the Iñupiat in Alaska, the Inuvialuit in Canada, and the Kalaallit in Greenland) live way up in the freezing Arctic, where the temperature can go as low as minus 22 degrees Fahrenheit. It's super important for these people to stay warm and not lose any heat. That's why they use special animal furs that nature made just for this purpose. The reason these furs are fluffy and shaggy is because there's a lot of air trapped between the hairs. This air doesn't mix with the cold air outside, so it keeps the wearer nice and warm. It's like having a cozy blanket around them all the time.

### Divers and surfers

Divers and surfers also protect themselves from the cold with an insulating layer. This time it is hidden in a wetsuit made of a special material called neoprene. Water is unable to get through this material, but that doesn't mean there is no water between the diver's body and the neoprene. A little water seeps through the seams, but you will notice how tight wetsuits are. Thanks to this, the layer of water on the body is very thin and the diver quickly heats it up. The important thing is that they don't have to heat it with their body over and over again – once is enough. The layer doesn't come into contact with the surrounding water, so it doesn't cool down, which is why it heats the divers up.

> Urgh, how are you supposed to squeeze into this?!

special neoprene material

skin

layer of water

20

## People who live in the desert

It is interesting that the inhabitants of the desert don't use a layer of air in their clothing to protect them from the heat. Instead, they have come up with their own trick where they try to keep the air constantly flowing around their bodies to cool them down. This is why their clothing is very loose. Another strange thing is that they often wear black, which we already know attracts the heat from the sun's rays. But the fact that their robes are loose and warmed-up actually helps people who live in the desert. The robes work a bit like a chimney, helping the air around their bodies to flow out even more quickly.

A robe and air conditioning all in one – what a bargain!

## Firefighters

A firefighter's uniform is really special because it has to withstand high temperatures during fires. It is made of three main layers. The first layer is closest to the body. It helps to move the firefighter's sweat away from their body. The middle layer protects them from the extreme temperatures. It's designed to trap a lot of air, just like an Inuit's fur coat. The surface layer is very tough. It protects the firefighter from sharp objects and other injuries.

The fire can't get through the cloth, and the miraculous fire-resistant suit can still breathe!

Help! Save me!

Do you ever help your parents in the kitchen? Do you stir or chop? Or maybe you've even cooked a meal by yourself? Cooking can sometimes seem as complicated as science, but it's fun to conduct experiments that you can all eat afterwards.

CHANGES OF STATE

### Dancing droplets

If a little water drops onto a hot pan, you can expect it to evaporate immediately, end of story. But the opposite is true. The droplets will run and dance on the surface. When the pan is really hot, the lower part of each droplet quickly evaporates. This forms a pillow of steam at the bottom, which protects the upper part of the droplets. It takes a while for the heat to get to it. And thanks to this pillow of steam, the droplets can slide around on the pan without sticking to it. And a wonderful spectacle will happen!

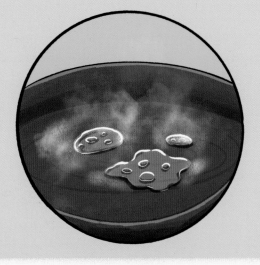

*Careful with that hot pot!*

FLOWING

### From water to steam

Puddles of rainwater and clothes on a clothesline both dry. It doesn't happen straight away, though, and sometimes it takes a long time. This is because with every wet thing, only the water on the surface can jump out and become vapor. And if the surrounding temperature climbs over 200 degrees Fahrenheit, then there's a real commotion! The water begins to evaporate from everywhere all at once with a crazy bubbling.

*We sleep quietly as ice...*

*Now we are almost free...*

water molecules

melting

heating

## Clouds above a pot

Have you ever made a cloud? What, never? Maybe you did without even knowing it. We often say that steam is coming out of a pot, but what we are really looking at is mist or a small cloud. We wouldn't actually be able to see steam (evaporated water) because it is completely transparent. Whereas that nice fog above a hot pot is visible, and the higher it rises, the more it is cooled down by the surrounding air. Gradually, the steam turns into small water droplets that together form a cloud.

## Self-stirring soup

When heating up a pot of soup, we put it on the stove and heat it from below. But why? Wouldn't it work just as well if we heated the pot from the side or maybe from above? Yes, this would also work, but much more slowly, because heat rises. When we heat the water from the bottom, it expands and rises to the surface. Cold water sinks to the bottom. In this way, soup stirs itself and heats up more quickly. It's similar to hot air in a room.

Hooray, f-r-e-e-e-d-o-m!

boiling

## Careful, it's hot

While we're cooking food, we heat up many other things along the way. First of all, the hot stove heats up the pan, which is made of metal, which can heat up quickly all the way through. This is useful, because whatever we put in the pot will heat up not only from the bottom but also from the sides. However, when we want to take the pot off the stove and move it somewhere else, the handle is burning hot, so we need to wear oven gloves. That's why it's better if the handles are made of plastic or wood rather than metal – that way, they don't heat up so quickly.

## It's cooking

When you are getting ready to make some food, many questions come to mind. Should you boil, fry, roast, or stew? And which kitchen utensils will you need? The main thing is to keep calm and enjoy it!

## Boiling point

The temperatures at which water boils and freezes were chosen by a man named Mr. Celsius. On his scale, he marked them as 100°C and 0°C and then he used them to determine the temperature of everything else. However, many people, especially in America, use a different scale called Fahrenheit. Water freezes at 32°F and boils at 212°F. In both cases, the temperature of the water stays the same – we just record it using different numbers. It's okay if we use different units, as long as we all know what is meant by them.

## Water under pressure

There's a trick to getting water to continue to boil at temperatures over 200 degrees Fahrenheit. It can be done under pressure! When you enclose it in a pot with a special tight-fitting lid that doesn't allow even a wisp of steam to escape, more and more steam will build up. This puts pressure on the water, making it boil hotter. You can cook meat or vegetables in a pressure cooker much more quickly without having to use oil. But it also works the other way around. If we take a trip to some high mountains, suddenly there isn't so much air above us. This means there is less pressure on us and so water boils at a lower temperature than we are used to. That is why it takes mountaineers in the Himalayas much longer to cook their meals. So if you're going on a high-altitude expedition, taking the kind of beans that need to be cooked for hours is maybe not the best idea.

A good mountaineer always finds a way.

It's been boiling for two hours and it's still not ready...

Food's ready. Yum!

PRESSURE COOKER 3000

## Lids and suction cups

It's not a good idea to wander away from a pot of boiling water. During the process of boiling, it will start to merrily take on a life of its own. When water turns into steam, it expands a lot. One droplet can produce enough steam to fill a glass. When you put a lid on a pot, it's not long before the steam can no longer fit in the pot. And unless the lid has a hole in it, the steam has to get out some other way – which is why it starts to rattle about...

### AIR DOESN'T LIKE EMPTINESS

Take a lid (one without holes in it) off of a boiling pot and put it on the kitchen countertop. You'll quickly discover that it's impossible to lift. It's completely stuck to the surface. What's holding it there so firmly? The air around it is pressing down on it. When the steam under the lid cools, small droplets of water reform. Suddenly it's much emptier below the lid than it was before. The surrounding air tries to fill the vacuum and get inside. But when it has no way to get in, it just presses down on the lid from all sides.

### DO YOU FEEL UNDER PRESSURE?

All suction cups work in a similar way. Most of them are flexible so it's easy to squeeze the air out from underneath them. Air can squeeze things pretty hard. It may be light, but there's a big layer of it above us. It pushes down on us with the same force as an adult standing on your hand.

212°F      356°F

## To boil or to fry?

Water can't have a higher temperature than the one at which it boils. However, sometimes during cooking that temperature isn't high enough. What do we do then? Try as we might, we can't make soup that little bit hotter. It would all evaporate before it reached that point. But we can make use of this fact and cook with steam instead of water. The food will be ready sooner and it will also keep more of its vitamins. But please be careful – hot steam can scald you much more badly than boiling water.

Another possibility is to abandon water altogether and use oil instead. It can be heated to a higher temperature, so food can be cooked faster by frying rather than boiling it. However, we mustn't overdo it with the frying temperature... Although the outside of the food will cook quickly when deep-frying, the inside takes a while longer. A half-burnt, half-raw lunch certainly wouldn't taste very nice... Deep-frying does have its advantages though. For example, have you ever tried deep-fried ice cream?

Suction cups are great...

...for your smartphone...

...or for an oven glove...

11:30

0.3 miles

...for example, for a toothbrush...

Cooking is all about working with heat. To keep food fresh for a long time and keep it from going bad, we keep it cool. And to make it taste nice, we might heat it up in a pot or in the oven or on a frying pan. How do these different heating methods work, though? And how can we cool hot food down again?

**CONVERSION OF ENERGY**

## A fridge heats

A fridge creates cold space inside itself. To keep our food cool, it has to somehow get rid of all the heat we don't want inside it. It's kind of like a little machine that moves heat around, just like a pump. This machine takes the heat from inside the fridge and sends it away through some special coils at the back. But here's the interesting part: the heat doesn't just disappear. If we want the inside of the fridge to be cold, then the back of the fridge needs to be hot. That's why it's good to keep the fridge slightly away from the wall so the heat can escape safely.

**CHANGE OF STATE**

## A bottle in the freezer

Everyone feels like having a cool drink once in a while. So what's the fastest way to chill a glass bottle with liquid in it? It's definitely not a good idea to put it in the freezer. If you leave it there for too long, the water in the bottle will freeze. You might think: That *doesn't matter, I'll have ice cream instead of a drink*. But when water freezes, it expands quite a lot. This can even make the glass bottle crack, leaving the freezer full of broken glass.

**RADIATION**

## Water in a microwave oven

Microwave ovens are strange devices. They're great at heating up some foods and not so good with others. The main thing microwaves are good at is heating water. So dry pasta will remain pretty cold, while a cup of tea will heat up quickly.

Freezes inside...

Heats at the back...

Uh-oh. Shards of glass...

**ELECTRICITY**

Almost there...

And it's boiling!

## Electric cooker

In the past, people used to cook over a fire, and this didn't change in the days of gas cookers. But for a while now, people have also been cooking with electricity. It might sound strange, but we actually want the electricity to flow poorly and slowly through the electric hob – the part of the cooker where you place your pots and pans to cook food. The reason is that when the electricity flows poorly and slowly, it also creates a lot of heat. That's why when you lift up a pot from the cooker, you will see the red-hot coils underneath it.

## Induction cooker

The induction cooker is the weirdest of all the cookers. As with the electric cooker, there are also coils of wire in it, but here we want them to conduct electricity as best they can. An induction plate is like a magic stove that uses a special power called magnetism. It creates a special force field, just like a TV station or a Wi-Fi antenna. When you put the right pot on this special stove, it can trap this magic power, soak it in, and get really hot. So the pot gets hot, but the stove stays cool.

Sounds like
it's done boiling.

## Electric kettle

The same heating coils that are used in an electric hob are also found in a kettle. Unlike a cooker, though, a kettle can switch itself off. But how does a kettle know when the water is hot enough? This is the job of a small metal strip. It's actually two different metals joined together in one small dish. When this strip has heated up, it pops and bends the other way. This pushes a switch and the kettle stops boiling. When your parent or some other adult pours themselves some tea, pause for a moment and listen. You'll hear how it pops in the kettle. That was the metal going back to its original shape.

CLICK!

# How does a microwave oven work?

## How does it heat up food?

When we want to heat up food, we need to set its atoms and molecules (the tiny things that everything is made of) in motion. Atoms move very quickly in hot things and very slowly in cold things. When you put a pot on the stove, the fast atoms of the stove bump into the slow atoms of the pot, which gets them moving. From the outside, we can see it in the way the pot slowly begins to heat up. A microwave oven basically does the same thing, but in a different way. The microwaves in the oven are what we call electromagnetic waves. And just as the waves in the sea can rock a boat on the surface and move around clumps of seaweed, so electromagnetic waves can tug at and move around the food's atoms and molecules. So the microwave oven is pulling at the atoms of your dinner thanks to electrical forces!

Before heating up:

Blaarrgh, this is bo-o-o-ring...

In the microwave oven:

Two hundred and twenty-one, two hundred and twenty-two! No slacking off for us!

## Atoms

Take a look at all the different things around you. If you began to cut them up into the smallest possible pieces, you would eventually get to the atoms. In Greek the word *atomos* means it can't be divided any further. That's why you can't keep cutting things into smaller pieces forever. But an atom actually consists of even smaller particles. We call them protons, neutrons, and electrons. Electrons can escape from atoms quite easily. When this happens and they move through a piece of wire, for example, we say there is an electric current flowing through the wire.

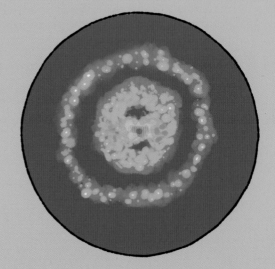

This is the best image of an atom that scientists have captured. But all we can see are the electrons. The nucleus (the center of the atom) is so tiny it can't be seen – not even with the best microscopes.

## Why does the food spin around?

When you put a wave inside a box, very strange things start to happen to it. Sometimes, the wave is really powerful and makes a big impact. Other times, it's hardly there at all. You can try this with water in the bathtub. If you're good at it, you can create huge waves in one part, but in another part, the water will stay completely still.

The microwaves in our microwave oven act in the same way. In some places they are strong and they get the atoms of the food moving around so that it heats up quickly. In other places, though, the microwaves are weak and the food stays cold. The easiest way to fix this is to turn the food around slowly until everything is warm and ready to eat.

## Anything but metal

In metal objects, such as a spoon, nothing can keep the electrons in the atoms. They move through metal as they please. When the microwaves start tugging on them, they move around so much that they jump right out of the spoon. When there are enough electrons moving through the air in the microwave like this, we can see sparks flashing from the outside. But these flashes are dangerous and can cause fires. So no experiments like that, please!

## The bowl is hot but the food is cold

This happens with some kinds of ceramic bowls. It's very simple. When a microwave spreads throughout the microwave oven, it hits the bowl first. Two things can then happen, depending on the type of bowl. Either it can let the microwave pass through towards the food or it can swallow up the microwave's energy and stop it from getting through. If your dish is good at gobbling up microwaves, then the food won't get heated up. It's a bit like wearing sunglasses and then complaining that it's dark!

How do you make waves in a microwave oven?

## A chocolate experiment

You can find out for yourself where your microwave oven heats up food the most and where it heats it the least. This is really quite a tasty experiment! First, put some grated chocolate on a plate. Next, put it in the microwave so that it doesn't spin around. Switch on the microwave and see if the chocolate has melted anywhere. If not, try microwaving it a while longer. The chocolate will only melt in some places and in others it will still be cold.

Grate the chocolate onto a plate...

This is how the plate looks before going into the microwave oven...

6 cm

...and this is how it looks afterwards!

## Fog on the mirror

It's a struggle. You take a shower, wash your hair, and then you want to comb it. Except you can't see a thing in the mirror because it's all steamed up. A bathroom is full of steam and a mirror is cold, so when the hot steam hits it, it turns into small droplets. What can be done about it? If your hair's wet and you've got a comb in your hand and you're in a hurry, you can try blowing on the mirror for a while with a hairdryer. Or give it a wipe.

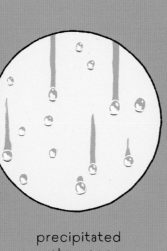

precipitated water vapor

The bathroom is like a small watery kingdom inside your home. You can explore the water in a bathtub for hours and get clean at the same time. But there are other interesting things to be found here too, such as a mirror and a tap.

> Why is it that my mirror image always raises the opposite hand?

> Who's controlling it?!

## A mirror image

We know that a mirror reverses an image. But how does it actually do this? After all, we don't see ourselves upside-down in it. When you raise your right hand, it looks in the mirror like you're raising your left hand. And yet it's still your right hand. When you point to the right, your image will also point to the right, as the mirror doesn't flip the image from side to side. So if you point forwards, straight in front of you, your image points at you. It almost looks like magic!

## A bath plug

Some bathtubs have a small piece of rubber that blocks the plughole so we can take a bath. But sometimes this plug is impossible to pull out – it's held in place with tremendous force. Whenever this happens, it's because a small vacuum has developed below the plug in the pipes. More importantly, there is a lot of water above the plug and all of that water is pressing down on the plug. It doesn't matter how long or wide the bath is. What matters is how deep the water in the bath is.

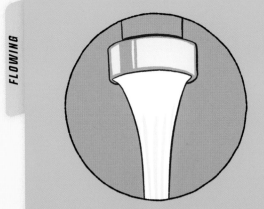

## The water flows from the tap

When you run a bath, pay attention to the shape of the water flowing from the tap. You can get a good view of it from above the bath because the water falls into it from pretty high up. The stream of water flows downwards, gradually becoming narrower. That's because you cannot squeeze water. If you let it flow throw a narrower pipe, the water would have to speed up to keep from collecting somewhere. It also works the other way around. When water speeds up as it falls, the stream becomes narrower. And it will keep getting thinner until it splits into individual droplets.

## A shaving mirror

Sometimes there are also smaller mirrors in a bathroom where you see yourself enlarged. This can come in handy if you want to put on make-up or pluck a hair from your nose. A shaving mirror can't be straight – it has to curve inwards like a water bowl. If you don't have this kind of mirror in your bathroom, you can try looking at yourself in a spoon or a metal ladle. You'll see that the curved shiny surface really does magnify the image!

Mirror, mirror on the wall, who's the toothiest of them all?

**WATER PRESSURE**

31

# Why does our hair stand up when we comb it?

By Zeus's beard, this is a peculiar stone!

No one's got a hairstyle like this.

Thales of Miletus

## An electric comb

Combing your hair can sometimes be a real problem. Occasionally, hair can get so tangled that it's almost better to just get it cut. And then there are days when you comb and comb your hair and it stands up on end as though drawn towards your comb by some invisible force. This is because of static electricity, also known as friction electricity.

### WHERE DOES ELECTRICITY COME FROM?

Friction really can produce electricity. This has been known for a long time – in fact, since Ancient Greece. Thales of Miletus was cleaning a piece of amber on his toga when he noticed how the material and the stone were attracted to each other. The Greek word for amber is *elektron*, which is why we use the word *electricity* today.

### AN ELECTRIFYING HAIRCUT

Only some combs can charge your hair. These are usually plastic ones, but a glass one also does the trick,

though it doesn't work at all with metal combs. It's also easier to electrify freshly washed or fine hair. People with thicker, coarser hair have to bring out the big guns. For example, an inflated balloon is great at producing electricity when it comes into contact with hair – although combing with it is a bit of a struggle! To get back to the plastic comb, though, why is it that it attracts hair so much? When you comb your hair, you give it one charge while your hair has the opposite charge. These opposite charges attract one another, which is why your hair sticks to the comb. All of the hairs have the exact same charge, and because like charges repel each other, our hair suddenly doesn't want to stick together at all.

### ELECTRICITY IN YOUR SWEATER

You feel the exact same static electricity when you pull a woollen sweater over your head. You might even be able to hear a quiet crackling as the charges jump around between your hair and the wool. You might also see small sparks in pitch darkness.

# The mystery of the stinky pipe

The water in the siphon prevents the smell from spreading.

## How to stop waste from smelling

Under every bathroom sink you'll find a strangely twisted pipe. At first the pipe points downward, but then it goes up again. Then it bends downward again before heading horizontally into the wall. Why such a complex shape? Why not just put a straight pipe in there? The reason is because this piece of twisted pipe makes sure that we don't smell the stench from the sewage system!

### THE SIPHON

This twisted pipe is called a siphon. The way it works is super simple. A little water always remains in the lower bend. If you'd like to know how much is there, you don't even have to dismantle the sink. The water level can't reach higher than the straight section of the pipe, which leads into the wall. And it's this small amount of water that creates a water barrier that separates the air in the bathroom from the air in the sewer. You'll find a similar bend or siphon under every drain – under the kitchen sink, under the bath and even behind the toilet.

### TANTALUS'S GOBLET (THOSE GREEKS AGAIN)

If you were to turn a siphon upside-down, it would start to work in an extremely interesting way. In Ancient Greece, they used this principle to produce a special goblet. If you poured wine in it up to a given mark, you could drink it in peace. However, if you poured in more wine, the whole goblet would spill out onto the floor. It didn't pay to be greedy in Ancient Greece.

## An experiment with charging

You should definitely try this experiment in the bathroom! Charge an inflated balloon or a ruler by rubbing it on your hair. Then get a thin stream of water flowing from the tap. Bring the balloon close to it without touching the stream. Attracted to the balloon, the water should bend in an arc towards it. It might surprise you, too, how much it actually bends. Water loves to stick to things that have an electric charge because its molecules can easily move and position themselves close to charged objects.

Wow, an electrified balloon attracts water like a magnet!

# OUTSIDE THE HOUSE

You will also find a lot of physics on the roof, on the walls, and even inside them. Try drawing a picture of a nice little house. Does it have a chimney, windows, and a door? But that's definitely not everything, is it? Do you know all of the nooks and crannies in a house and how they work?

## The chimney

Have you ever wondered why chimneys go up? When you fire up a stove, the air inside heats up, expands, and starts to move upwards, along with the gases produced from burning things. We call this hot, dirty air smoke. As it rushes up the chimney, it creates a draft that draws fresh air into the stove. The higher the chimney, the better the draft. And in order for it to draw properly, the smoke has to be much hotter than the air outside.

## Circuit breaker

Do you have a junction box in front of your house too? Here the electrical current that leads into your home is split into different circuits. Some devices need less of the current, so they have a lower electrical load, while others use more of it. But watch out – electric overload can easily set something on fire. If you decide to do the ironing, put on a load of washing, heat up spaghetti in the microwave, and boil water in the kettle for tea all at the same time, it's probably not the best idea. Fortunately, every home is protected by a circuit breaker, which limits the amount of current being drawn. If you plug in too many appliances, the clever circuit breaker switches off the electricity...

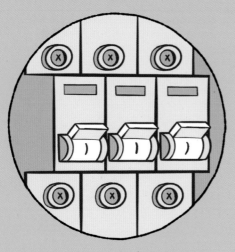

... so the house doesn't burn down.

## Solar panels

Solar panels draw energy from the sun. Have you noticed that there are more and more of them these days? Where do you see them the most often? The best place for solar panels is the sunny side of the roof, where they don't get in anyone's way. Although they might not be the nicest decoration for a roof, they can provide hot water or even make a home self-sufficient with electricity. In this case, efficiency wins over beauty.

## A liquid thermometer

This type of thermometer usually contains mercury or colored alcohol. Both liquids are sensitive to the surrounding temperature and change their volume with each change in temperature. When it's cold the level falls, and when it's hot it goes up. You can easily find out the exact temperature by checking the (attached) scale. Mercury is a silver metal which is a liquid at room temperature. However, mercury vapours are poisonous, which is why mercury thermometers have been replaced by the safer alcohol-based ones.

How many degrees is it?

## Lightning rod

Most of us can't imagine living in a house without electricity. However, there is one electrical charge that no one wants in their house – lightning. That's why most houses have a protective iron spike on the roof with a cable leading down to the ground. It's not an antenna but a path prepared for lightning – a so-called lightning rod. It's always easiest for lightning to strike the highest and sharpest point. It then glides smoothly down into the ground, where the extra charge is harmlessly dispersed, allowing us to stay safe.

## Insulation

The insulation in a home works as though the whole house was wrapped in a giant warm coat. It's there to make sure the warmth inside doesn't escape and the cold doesn't get in, and the other way round. Thanks to proper insulation, we have better control over the room temperature. Like our clothing, home insulation also makes use of a layer of air – to help us we have materials with a lot of air in them, such as polystyrene, fiberglass, foam, and even straw. Air is the very best insulator there is.

proper insulation

# Saving energy...

Whenever you want to do something useful, it takes effort and energy. This is also true at home. Drinking a cup of hot tea, watching a film on TV, surfing the internet, or just having a light on in your bedroom – all of this takes energy, and energy costs money. How much energy does a household need and where does it use it the most?

## Four hours of your life...

It takes a lot of energy just to heat up water. It's such a big and important number that it can even be used to measure energy. You sometimes find on food packaging how much energy you get if you eat it. Often this is all shown in calories. And one calorie is in fact the very amount of energy needed to heat up a liter of water by one degree Celsius. Is that a lot or a little? Just imagine, the energy needed to bring a liter of tap water to the boil would give your body enough energy to live off for four hours!

## The biggest energy guzzlers

As well as water, we also use a lot of electrical energy at home. On each appliance it says how much energy it guzzles. Among the greediest are the cooker, the washing machine, the kettle, and the fridge. Once again, these are appliances that heat up or cool water. But a lot of energy is also consumed by your computer or TV. A gaming computer can easily rival a washing machine in terms of its consumption.

## Let's not waste energy

Every bit of energy consumed costs something. It's not smart to waste it on something you don't need or don't want. You'd be amazed how often we waste energy at home on appliances that are switched on but doing nothing, just waiting there until we need them. Televisions and mobile-phone chargers are often left on standby mode. Another example is we might fill up a whole kettle even though we only need enough water for one cup of tea.

Washing only a single pair of socks wastes a lot of energy.

The heat won't get out this way.

## Keeping the heat in

It would be just as big a waste if energy was to escape from our warm home. To prevent this, we use insulation. Still, it's worth looking at where we lose energy from our home. We've already mentioned that the warm air in a house always rises. That's why it's warmest under the roof. The warmer it is in the house and the colder it is outside, the easier it is for the heat to escape through the roof. This is why, when insulating a home, it pays to start with the roof.

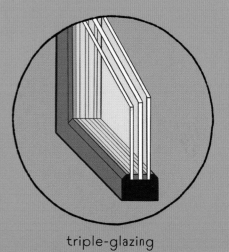

triple-glazing

Heat escapes from our houses through every hole in the wall, in particular the biggest ones, such as windows and doors. That's why it's a good idea to insulate them with several layers of glass. If we do this, the heat will only escape through the window frame, while the glass panes won't let much heat out. But what if we want to air out the room properly from time to time? After all, we need fresh air as well. To make sure we lose as little heat as possible, we air out the room briefly but thoroughly with the windows wide open. And then quickly close them again... *Brrr!*

## How to save energy

We heat up water at home surprisingly often. Hot water also flows inside many heating systems. Even the hot water from the tap had to be heated up somewhere. And it would be a terrible shame if all that warming energy were to go to waste, for example because of something as simple as forgetting that you've just run a hot bath.

# 9 IN THE GARAGE

In the garage, we try to make things stronger, measure things as accurately as possible, and use the best materials. It really is amazing how much patience and ingenuity can be found in an ordinary workshop!

## Hard and soft

There is one basic rule: the tool must be harder than the material you are working with. The saw must bite into the wood and cut the individual fibers. If the opposite was true, you wouldn't get much cutting done. A soft sawblade would soon become blunt and get ground down until it was completely smooth. This is why tools are usually made from very hard materials, like hardened steel – it is very hard but also brittle. And so a steel drill bit tends to break rather than bend. But you can find even harder tools: titanium, corundum, and even diamond.

Argh! Come on, budge!

@#$! Still nothing

## Who tightened this?

You can't loosen a nut and bolt with your fingers – it takes greater force. Wrenches, pliers, and screwdrivers all turn similarly, but they also increase the distance between your hand and the place where you are turning the screw. This is because a longer lever (meaning a tool that helps us lift or move things) increases your strength. So the next time you have problems loosening a nut, try using a longer and longer wrench.

Much better.

## Sharp and blunt

We think of a nail as something sharp. But in reality, the tips of nails are blunt. When they are being made, a machine cuts off the end of some wire to create a typical nail tip. A screw, on the other hand, has to be made sharp in order to cut a thread into the wood, which we then have to unscrew it from. However, there has to be space in the wood for either the nail or the screw. If you don't want the wood to splinter, it's a good idea to drill a small hole for the nail or the screw.

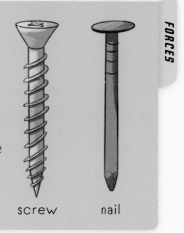

screw          nail

## Measuring with a saw

Measure twice and cut once... But you don't always have to reach for a ruler. Sometimes all you need is an ordinary one-handed saw. You can use it to draw a straight line, but did you know it can also measure angles? Its handle is shaped in such a way that you can easily measure right angles and 45-degree angles. So the next time you want to cut a straight piece of wood or make a picture frame, a saw and a pencil are all you need.

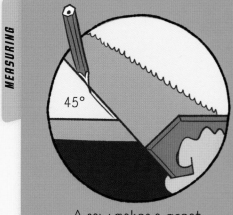

A saw makes a great protractor.

## A tape measure

At the end of a tape measure, you'll find a small metal hook that can move ever so slightly. If you want to measure the length of a wooden board, you can easily attach the tape measure to one end and pull. But if you want to measure a room from wall to wall, you push the tape measure against the wall.

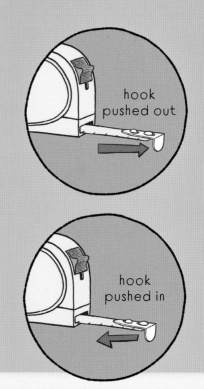

hook pushed out

hook pushed in

## Get out of that hole, nail

When hammering a nail, all it takes is one wrong hit and the nail is bent. How do you get it out of the wood? Usually it's not enough just to pull at it. You can use pliers, but there's a little trick that comes in handy. Don't just pull at the nail – try to turn it slightly. The friction that is making it harder for the nail to come out will have to work in more directions at once as you twist it. It will then be that much easier to pull it out.

# Screwing, drilling, and cutting...

## Screws and nuts

A long time ago, all screws had only one groove in them – a straight one. And all screwdrivers were the same, just of different sizes. But the workers in Henry Ford's factory noticed that after a while the screwdriver always slipped out of the straight groove, which caused problems. And so various improvements soon appeared – screwdrivers in the shape of a pyramid and screws with the same groove, as well as screwdrivers in the shape of a cross or a star.

### SCREW HEADS

Today there are so many differently shaped screws that we have a special screwdriver for each one at home. But you'll always find ones with one groove, a cross, or a star made from three grooves. If you can brace the screwdriver against more grooves, you can tighten and loosen with more force. But if a screw is too tight and you can't loosen it, it helps to push

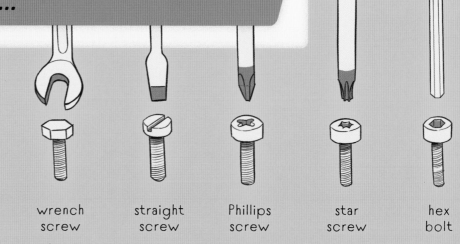

wrench screw    straight screw    Phillips screw    star screw    hex bolt

into it The more pressure you put on it from above, the more securely it stays in the screw, allowing you to twist more. Sometimes, though, the head of the screw is so worn that the screwdriver has nothing to dig into. In that case, you can try putting a piece of rubber band between the screw and the screwdriver. Then the screwdriver will bite into the rubber and hopefully won't slip anymore.

### RIGHT TIGHTENS, LEFT LOOSENS

The way screws are loosened or tightened isn't random. It's because

you are able to twist with more force with your right hand when you twist clockwise – and most people are right-handed ( the left hand is stronger in the opposite direction). So you tighten to the right and loosen to the left. However, there are also screws and nuts that have the thread running the other way. They're usually used to hold something that has to turn in this direction, such as a crank or a fan propellor. If these appliances had an ordinary thread, the nut would come loose as it turned.

Tighten
to the right.

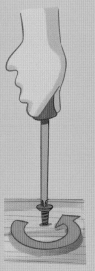

Loosen
to the left.

## Warming up at work

It's not just you who gets hot when you're working hard. When you hammer a nail into wood, you can see right away that it doesn't really want to go in. That's because the material of the wood is too tight. So you hit the nail with a big, heavy hammer to knock a hole through it. But with each blow, it only goes in a little bit further. So where has all the energy from your hammer gone? It can't just have disappeared! After a few hits, try touching the head of the nail. Do you feel how hot it is? That's where the energy from your hammering went. Now try hammering the nail until it's flat as a pancake!

Almost everything in the workshop heats up in the same way. A screw has to be forced into wood as well. When you're screwing it in, you can sometimes hear a creaking sound as the screw eats into the wood. Similarly, when you're drilling a hole into a wall, the drill forces a path through the brick, cutting away a piece of it with every turn. Soon it is so hot you could burn yourself on it. When cutting a wooden plank, the friction heats up the sawblade and the wood. The wood can even start to turn black and heat up with smoke.

Ouch!

This new screwdriver really is something! The screws don't slip at all...

Messing around in the garden at Grandma and Grandpa's is a lot more fun than at home. Try keeping your eyes and ears open. You're bound to come up with tons of interesting questions you'd never think of at home.

**FLOWING**

## Watering the garden

On scorching summer days, it's fun to water the plants in the garden, as well as each other. But what if the water pressure is too low and the lazy trickle of water won't spray as far as you want it to? All you have to do is slightly squeeze the end of the hose or partly block it with your finger and the water will spray more quickly and forcefully. The smaller the opening it has to go through, the faster it flows. It doesn't want a traffic jam to form in the pipe!

**WATER PRESSURE**

## Flowing uphill

The weather can be really changeable. Heavy rain one moment and then not a drop for ages. But plants need to drink constantly. That's why it's a good idea to have a barrel in the garden to collect all the rainwater. But what do you do when one barrel is completely full? You can place another one beside it and pump the water into it.

Transferring all those gallons of water into buckets would take a long time. But there's a smart way around it! All it takes is a hose and a little skill. To completely fill the hose up with water, suck it like a straw. Next, simply place the end of the hose in the empty barrell. Then, as long as the water level in the full barrel is at least slightly higher than in the empty barrel, the water will flow from the full barrell into the empty barrel all by itself, even though the water is being sent uphill and then downhill. In the end, the water levels always even out.

Better hold on to me.

Nature will even it out for us.

full barrel

empty barrel

## A picture experiment

A magnifying glass can be used to enlarge writing in a book, but also to project something – for example, a picture onto paper. Borrow a magnifying glass, get a sheet of paper, and go over to the window. Slowly move the glass away from the paper. At some point, a small, colored window will appear on the paper. Try to make the image as sharp as you can. You'll notice that the tiny window image appears upside down. We have a similar magnifying glass in our eye, and images are formed in it upside down. But the brain is incredibly clever and it is constantly turning everything we see the right way around.

## Climbing without falling

If you want to pick an apple from a tree, you might need a ladder. Finding the right angle to get up and down safely, though, can be a bit of an artform. If the angle is too vertical, you could tip backwards. If the angle is too flat, the ladder could easily slide out from under you and you could end up on the ground. But there's a way to position the ladder so it's as stable as possible. It just takes a bit of practice. In the end, it's easiest if someone holds the ladder from below.

Too horizontal...     Too vertical...     Just right!

## Rapid ripening

Fruit and vegetables can't be grown everywhere all year long. If someone from a colder region wants to enjoy their own home-grown produce, they might choose to build a greenhouse. The glass walls of the greenhouse let the sun's rays through, which means that even in wintertime the plants can get enough light and heat. Although a little bit of the heat escapes through the glass, because the wind doesn't get into the greenhouse most of it stays there. In summertime, people often find it unbearable in a greenhouse, but peppers and tomatoes love it and ripen much more quickly.

Peppers and tomatoes ripen beautifully in a greenhouse

## When the senses fail

Old people are full of wisdom gathered during their lifetimes. Many of them use a walking stick, some of them wear glasses, and some have hearing aids. These things help them overcome the challenges of old age, when our bodies often need a helping hand, and it's quite interesting to see how they can help.

What would I do without my trusty reading glasses?

### How does the eye work?

The eye allows you to see shapes and colors and to tell how far away things are. It's a clever instrument and yet it's not all that complicated. When light enters your eye, the first thing it comes across is a lens. This works like a magnifying glass, which our eyes flatten or thicken slightly using tiny muscles. This is how we get the world around us into focus. When we look into the distance, the lens has to focus on the distance and the muscles have to flatten it more. However, when we look at something right in front of us, the muscles make the lens thicker. Once it gets past the lens, the light gradually passes through the whole eye, which is filled with a transparent liquid, until it reaches the back wall, where it forms a tiny picture of what we are seeing. The back wall of the eye is full of cells, which then send the light image on to the brain. And all of this is happening so fast that you're not even aware of the individual images and you see them as one continuous stream of images.

A wonderful invention, these glasses! Which brings me to the question – how do we humans actually see?

### Why do we wear glasses?

Some people are unable to focus the image in their eye properly. For example, their eyes can't make their lenses round enough or flat enough, or they have a slightly oval-shaped eye. Then they have to wear glasses to help them to focus. Glasses are basically just lenses – glass that has a special shape that we call either convex or concave.

**A convex lens** is like a magnifying glass – it has glass which is wider in the middle and thinner at the edges. It is usually worn by older people who have trouble seeing close up. When reading a newspaper, they'll hold it as far away as possible in order to focus. They can't make the lens in their eyes very round and so they have another lens in their glasses to help them.

**Concave lenses** are ground in the opposite way. They are thicker at the edges and thinner in the middle. A concave lens doesn't function as a magnifying glass because it can't concentrate the light – instead, it scatters it sideways. It is mainly used by young people, who often have poor long-distance vision. They can't focus on distant signs or the school blackboard. The lens in their eye can't flatten properly, so the opposite shape of lens is used.

 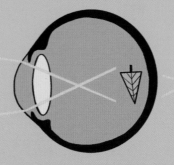  

Hey, look, a tree!

The eye turns the image of the tree upside down.

But our brain...

...can deal with it.

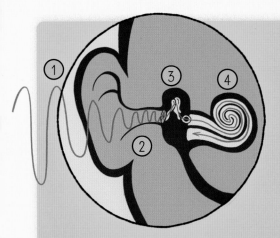

1. sound, 2. eardrum,
3. hammer and anvil,
4. auditory cells in the cochlea

## How does the ear work?

The journey that sounds take before you know that you're hearing them is quite a long one. First, notice how the ear is shaped like a funnel. This helps to transport more sounds into the ear from your surroundings and to amplify the sound. In fact, if you put a rolled-up paper cone to your ear, you will hear sounds a bit louder. Sound is basically just vibrating air. And just as there is a membrane in a microphone that is made to vibrate by vibrating air, there is a vibrating membrane in the ear called the eardrum. This makes tiny bones in the ear vibrate, which in turn cause a special fluid to vibrate. And in this "ear water" there are cells that dance about according to the size and speed of the sound wave that has reached them. They then send information about this to the brain. Then – and only then – do you finally hear sound!

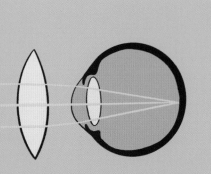

A convex lens corrects far-sightedness.

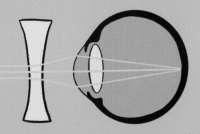

A concave lens corrects near-sightedness.

And a filter (from sunglasses) blocks the sun's rays.

## Why older people sometimes have trouble hearing

As we get older, we often lose some of our hearing. As we age, though, it's mainly high-pitched sounds we stop being able to hear, and it's these that help us distinguish different voices. This is why older people sometimes have problems understanding. They might hear you talking, but they don't understand what you're actually saying. You would hear the same way if someone threw a fluffy blanket over your head or pulled your hat down over your ears. Some older people, though, do need to use a hearing aid. This helps them to amplify all of the sounds around them. Which is why you shouldn't shout at a person with a hearing aid, as the hearing aid will amplify your shouting and hurt their ears! A hearing aid is in fact a small microphone (which listens to the sound outside) linked to an earpiece (which is inserted into the ear and sends an amplified sound to it).

## Changes of state

The materials around us have various forms. For example, we know water as ice (when it freezes) or as steam (when it boils). Water, then, can be found in all three states – as a solid, liquid, or gas. And, like water, most of the materials around us can be found in all three states. If you heat up a material enough, it will melt to become a liquid. We can then heat this up until it evaporates and becomes a gas. We can cool a gas until it turns to liquid or even until it freezes into a solid material. In this book, though, we have focused on water because we come across it the most often and it is by far the most important in our lives.

## Conversion of energy

Sometimes people say they have no energy. Energy, though, can't just disappear. Instead, it changes into a different form. For example, you might use the energy in your muscles to do lots of work, to kick a ball, or to warm your hands by rubbing them together. We can't produce energy – we always have to get it from somewhere. We can use the energy given off by the sun, the energy from water flowing in a river, or even the energy stored in a bar of chocolate.

## Electricity

It would be impossible to imagine today's world without electricity. It heats our water, spins the blender, cools the fridge, and charges our cell phones. It is produced in power stations and then runs along cables to our homes. We know a lot about it today and we can use it to help us, but it took inventors and scientists a long time to figure all of this stuff out.

## Energy

We need energy at home for many different things – for lighting or for heating rooms or the water for a bath. This is why where we get our energy from and how it gets into our home is so important. We can all influence how much energy we use and what we use it for. And we can all influence where we get our energy from. It is important to find a balance between our consumption and respect for the environment.

## Flowing

Water, air, and electricity all flow – meaning they move in a steady current. In physics, anything that flows is called a fluid. Water can flow in a river or in a pipe. Air can rise when it is warm, it can blow like the wind, and we can use an airflow to vacuum at home.

## Forces

When we apply force in the right direction, we can move something, turn it, or even crush it. We use forces to interact with all the things around us, even if we don't exactly mean to. The Earth pulls at us, the chair pushes against us, and friction works against us when we're moving. But what if you want to rest for a while? On Earth, we are never completely free from forces. When these forces are in balance, though, we hardly notice they're there.

## Heating

Nature likes to keep things in balance. Thus, warm things heat things up while cooling themselves until the temperature is the same everywhere. How quickly this happens depends on the materials involved. Metals, for example, are excellent heat conductors, so a metal teaspoon quickly heats and cools. Wood, water, and air, on the other hand, are very poor heat conductors.

## Light

In order to see something, light has to enter our eyes, and not only directly from the sun, from a fire, or from a lamp. We can also see things that themselves do not shine. However, the light has to reflect from them into our eyes. Our eyes can cope with light from red, yellow, green, blue, and purple. This rainbow of colors contains even more colors, but the human eye cannot see them. We then no longer call it light but radiation.

## Measuring

If we want precise answers to our questions about size, then we have to start measuring. And the more precise the answer, the more precise the measurement we need. This is why scientists work hard to come up with better and better measuring instruments. However, even simple measuring – perhaps with an ordinary ruler – can be a science. You have to know what you're doing to avoid mistakes that might give the wrong results.

## Radiation

Light is a form of radiation, but there are many types of radiation we can't see. Even the heat from the sun is radiation. Or ultraviolet radiation, which gives us a tan. Or X-rays at the doctor's, which allow us to look at broken bones. There is radiation from a Wi-Fi signal or the radio, and it heats up our food in a microwave oven. Radiation is all around us, but it is more difficult to understand because our eyes can't see it.

## Senses

Our senses give us information about the world around us. We can see it, hear it, smell it, taste it, and touch it. In reality, we have more than these traditional five senses – for example, we can sense temperature and time. However, we rely upon sight and sound the most. This is why it can be difficult if these senses stop working either partially or completely. Fortunately, today we are able to fix many problems with sight and hearing.

## Structure

It is fascinating to look at the world of small things and even smaller things. But while it might seem as though this world has nothing in common with our own, the opposite is true. If we really want to understand why some things melt when we hold them in our hand, while others form beautiful crystals, and still others shine like silver, then we have to dive deep into the material itself. We have to investigate what it is made from and how it is structured.

## Water pressure

Just as our backpack might press on our shoulders, water can press on us too because it also has weight. The layer of water on the surface presses on the water just below it. They both then press on the water below and so on and so on, until the layer of water at the bottom has quite a weight on its back, so to speak. At the bottom, then, the water can really press hard on something. You might not notice this if you dive just under the surface, but deep-sea divers or sea creatures living at the bottom have to cope with water pressure.

## The Amazing Theatre of Physics

The Amazing Theatre of Physics is a group of people who make a living by showing other people experiments. We want people to notice the world around us and to be aware of the laws that govern it. After all, the world is all the more beautiful when you know how it works.

## THE AMAZING THEATRE OF PHYSICS

is an entertainment and educational group that performs science experiments in order to show people how the world around us works in a way that is fun and exciting. They're like magicians, only they explain how their tricks work. Having started performing in 2008, they travel around the world with their show, performing in a wide range of venues, from theaters, town squares, and schools to churches, synagogues, and retirement homes.

This work is based on their lifelong research and experience.

© B4U Publishing for Albatros,
an imprint of Albatros Media Group, 2024
5. května 1746/22, Prague 4, Czech Republic
Written by The Amazing Theatre of Physics
Illustrations © Tomáš Kopecký
Translated by Graeme Dibble
Edited by Scott Alexander Jones

www.albatrosbooks.com